World of Music

Latin America and the Caribbean

Andrew Solway

Heinemann
LIBRARY

Chicago, Illinois

© 2008 Heinemann Library
A division of Reed Elsevier Inc.
Chicago, Illinois

Customer Service 888-454-2279

Visit our website at www.heinemannraintree.com

Designed by Victoria Bevan and Philippa Baile
Illustrations by Jeff Edwards and Darren Lingard
Originated by Chroma Graphics (Overseas) Pte Ltd
Printed and bound in China

12 11 10 09 08
10 9 8 7 6 5 4 3 2 1

**Library of Congress Cataloging-in-Publication
Data**
Solway, Andrew.
   World of music : Latin America and the Caribbean
/ Andrew Solway.
      p. cm.
   Includes bibliographical references (p.   ) and index.
   ISBN 978-1-4034-9889-2 (library binding -
hardcover)
   1. Music--Latin America--History and criticism-
-Juvenile literature. 2. Music--Caribbean Area--
History and criticism--Juvenile literature. I. Title. II.
Title: Latin America and the Caribbean.

   ML199.S65 2007
   780.98--dc22
   2006100579

Acknowledgments
The publishers would like to thank the following
for permission to reproduce photographs: Alamy
Images pp. **11** (Anders Ryman), **19** (Ricardo Beliel/
BrazilPhotos), **20** (Barry Lewis), **38–39** (Alex Segre);
ArenaPAL/Jak Kilby p. **12**; Corbis pp. **31** (Royalty
Free), **4** (Reuters/Eliana Aponte), **6–7** (Charles
& Josette Lenars), **10** (Reuters/Pilar Olivares),
14 (Historical Picture Archive), **16** (Francoise de
Mulder), **17** (Stephanie Maze), **23** (Pablo Corral
Vega), **24–25** (Dennis Degnan), **34** (Colita), **37**
(Jeff Albertson), **42** (Reuters/Carlos Barria); Getty
Images/Time Life Pictures p. **29**; Kobal Collection
p. **32** (Dispatfilm/Gemma/Tupan); Jeffrey Chock
p. **43**; Lebrecht/Alastair Muir p. **26–27**; Redferns
pp. **9**, **33** (Michael Ochs Archives), **21** (David
Redfern), **36** (Ron Howard), **40–41** (Paul Bergen);
Reuters p. **35** (Claudia Daut).

Cover photograph of musician playing guitar in
Mexican *mariachi* band reproduced with permission
of Alamy Images/Rodolfo Arpia.

The publishers would like to thank Patrick Allen for
his assistance in the preparation of this book.

Every effort has been made to contact copyright
holders of any material reproduced in this book.
Any omissions will be rectified in subsequent
printings if notice is given to the publishers.

Contents

Some words will be printed in bold, **like this.** You can find out what they mean by looking in the glossary.

Welcome to Latin-American and Caribbean Music

There are many types of Latin-American and Caribbean music. You are sure to know some of them. You have probably heard **reggae** music, from Jamaica in the Caribbean. Reggae's booming bass lines and laid-back **rhythms** are popular worldwide. **Salsa** is another popular sound. This fast, brassy music is great to dance to.

Latin America and the Caribbean

Latin America includes those countries south of the United States where people speak Spanish, Portuguese, or French. These are sometimes known as Latin languages, which is why the area is called Latin America.

The Caribbean includes all the islands in the Caribbean Sea, between North and South America. The mainland countries Belize and Guyana are also part of the Caribbean.

In February, many Latin American and Caribbean countries celebrate with carnivals featuring music and dancing.

Mountains, plains, and rain forests

Central America, the Caribbean, and much of South America are warm, tropical areas. High mountains and volcanoes run through Central America, and many of the lowland areas of Central America are covered by rain forest.

Much of the northern part of South America is covered by the vast Amazon rain forest. There are also large areas of savanna (mixed grassland and trees). The Andes Mountains run along the western side of the continent. South of the rain forest, except for the Andes, much of the land is flat. There is a large area of grassland known as the pampas, and south of this is a semi-desert region.

This map shows South America, Central America, and Mexico (colored yellow), the Caribbean (colored orange), and the surrounding area.

Latin people

The people of Latin America come from three different continents. The first people to live there were **Amerindians**. The Amerindians included people such as the Olmecs, Maya, Aztecs, and Incas. These people built cities, temples, and roads.

Then, in 1492, Christopher Columbus arrived in South America from Europe. He claimed several islands in the Caribbean for King Ferdinand of Spain. By 1532 the Spanish and Portuguese had conquered (taken over) most of Latin America and the Caribbean. The Spanish brought their own music to the area, such as Spanish **folk** songs and dances, hymns, and other church music.

This wall painting is from a temple in Bonampak, Mexico. It is more than 1,000 years old. It shows Mayan musicians playing drums (center and left), and large, decorated shakers (right).

Ancient instruments

Before Columbus arrived in South America, we knew little about the music of the Caribbean Indians. However, some of the first Spanish explorers wrote about the music and dancing they found. At ceremonies called *areitos*, musicians played slit drums (hollow logs with an H-shaped slit in the top), shakers (maracas), and scrapers (*guiros*).

We know little about the music of the region before Europeans arrived. Many Amerindians were killed by Europeans, or died of disease. Because of this, much of their music was lost.

So many Amerindians died that there were not enough people left to grow food and do other types of work. To solve this problem, the Spanish and Portuguese brought slaves from Africa to work in the Caribbean and South America.

Between the 16th century and the 19th century, millions of Africans were taken to Latin America and the Caribbean. Many worked on plantations (large farms) and grew things like sugar, coffee, and rubber tree plants. These slaves brought African rhythms and **percussion** to their new homes.

Colonialism and independence

In the 17th and 18th centuries, many Caribbean islands and parts of South America were taken over by Great Britain, France, and the Netherlands. In the **colonies** they ruled, the British banned black people from playing African-style drum music.

The Africans in British colonies such as Jamaica and Trinidad adapted their music to be sung or played on Western-style instruments. This is why the music of places such as Jamaica and Trinidad is different from that of the rest of Latin America and the Caribbean.

This map shows the colonizer countries and the countries they ruled in the Caribbean, South America, and Africa. The colonizers and their colonies are shown in matching colors.

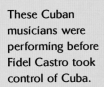
These Cuban musicians were performing before Fidel Castro took control of Cuba.

Independence

During the 19th century, most countries in Latin America and the Caribbean won independence (they began to rule themselves). The newly independent countries had all types of problems. Their governments changed often, and one group after another ruled the countries. In the 20th century, **dictators** ruled for many years in countries such as Nicaragua and Chile.

The different types of government affected how music developed in different countries. In Bolivia during the 1950s, for instance, the government encouraged more respect for Amerindians. This led to a new interest in the music of the Indians.

At about the same time, a **communist** government led by Fidel Castro took power in Cuba. Under Castro's government, Cuba became cut off from the rest of Latin America, and they began to develop other kinds of music.

Roots of the Music

Amerindian, African, and European people each brought their own types of music to Latin America and the Caribbean. These different types of music have mixed in many ways to produce Latin-American and Caribbean styles.

Amerindian music

Although there is no record of how Caribbean-Indian music sounded before the Spanish arrived, some instruments have survived. Maracas and *guíros* (shakers and scrapers) are part of the **percussion** in many types of Latin and Caribbean music.

In the Andean regions of South America, other types of Amerindian music have survived to the present day. In the 1500s, Spanish people traveling in South America wrote about hearing large bands of musicians playing drums and **panpipes**. The drums and panpipes had a type of musical conversation as the music moved back and forth between them. This type of music is still played at village fiestas (festivals) and **folk** music festivals in Peru and Bolivia.

Peruvian singer Anita Santivanez performs traditional Andean folk music. Here she sings at a concert in Lima.

The main instruments in traditional Andean music are flutes, drums, panpipes, and a small type of **mandolin** called a *charango*. *Charangos* used to be made from the shell of an **armadillo**. However, today armadillos are protected animals, so *charangos* are no longer made this way.

This man is playing his *charango* in the Andes, in Bolivia.

Fray Bartolomé

Fray Bartolomé de las Casas (1474–1524) was a Spanish priest who wrote many articles condemning the harsh way Spanish soldiers and rulers treated the Amerindians. In 1502 he visited Hispaniola (modern Haiti and the Dominican Republic). He wrote about the music and dancing of the **Taino Indians** that he saw on this visit: "And on this island what I could understand was that their songs, which they call *areytos*, were their history passed from person to person ... they passed three or four hours or more [singing and dancing] until the teacher or guide of the dance finished the history, and sometimes they went from one day to the next."

African music

Africa slaves brought many different types of music to Latin America and the Caribbean.

Most types of African music focus on **rhythm**. There are often two or more different rhythms being played at the same time. (American and European music usually has one clear beat that runs through a song or tune.) The different rhythms in African music weave in and out of each other to form complex, changing patterns. Cuban **rumba** music relies heavily on these types of complex rhythms, clearly showing its African roots.

African music is still popular throughout Latin America and the Caribbean. Farafina is a group from Burkina Faso in West Africa. They play traditional instruments such as *djembe* drums (bottom right), hourglass drums, and *balafons* (xylophones).

African songs often have an open-ended structure. The short, repeating patterns can be played over and over again. A singer or lead musician **improvises** (makes up new music) over this repeated background music. Much of the music played in Latin-American and Caribbean carnival processions is open-ended like African songs.

Many African songs have a call followed by a response. This is when one singer sings a line or verse of a song, and a chorus of singers then echoes the lead singer, or responds to the leader's song. **Salsa** and many other types of Latin music have call and response sections in the songs. In salsa music the singer usually sings a short section alone, then the chorus joins in. The chorus sings a phrase, then leaves a gap where the lead singer can improvise. Then the chorus repeats the phrase again.

Yoruba music

The Yoruba were a powerful group of African people living in what is now Nigeria. In the early 1800s, the Yoruba kingdom collapsed. Many Yoruba people were captured as other African people invaded their land. Thousands of them were sold as slaves.

Large numbers of Yoruba slaves were then brought to Cuba and Brazil. Because of this, certain types of Cuban and Brazilian music still have strong connections with Yoruba music. For instance, *santería* music uses *bata* drums, which are also played in Nigeria.

European music

The Europeans brought many types of music to Latin America and the Caribbean. European music is not usually open-ended like African music. Each piece has a clear beginning, middle, and end. The different singers and instruments play in **harmony** rather than all playing the same notes. (African songs also include harmonies, but they do not have such complex arrangements of different instruments and voices.)

This painting shows Cuban men and women performing a national *zapateado* dance in 1890. *Zapateado* comes from the Spanish word *zapatear*, which means to tap with the shoe.

ISLA DE CUBA.

EL ZAPATEADO.
The Zapateado (national dance)

One unusual element of Latin-American music that came from Europe was a type of Spanish poetry known as *décima*. In the 15th and 16th centuries, many Spanish poets wrote *décima* poems, and some of these poems were made into songs. *Décima* poetry died out in Spain many years ago. However, it lives on thousands of miles away in Latin America and the Caribbean, where many songs are written in this style.

The Europeans also brought many different instruments to Latin and Caribbean music. Instruments such as guitars, violins, and trumpets quickly became popular throughout the region.

Décima competitions

Décima poetry has very strict rules. This makes it difficult to write good *décima* poems. However, in many types of Latin and Caribbean music, the singers improvise *décima* verses as they go along. In some Puerto Rican villages, for instance, two rival bands play what is known as *jibaro* music for dancers in the village square. Each band has a singer, and they take turns to make up *décima* verses to the music. Whichever singer comes up with the best verses wins. These competitions can sometimes go on all night!

Amerindian instruments

Quena (flute)

Panpipes

Maracas (shakers)

Charango (mandolin)

Guiro (scraper)

African instruments

Congas (played with hands)

Timbales (played with wooden sticks)

Berimbau (musical bow)

Bongos (held between knees and played with hands)

Cowbells (hit with a stick)

European instruments

Trombone

Violin

Double bass

Button accordion

Trumpet

Guitar

Latin-American and Caribbean Religions

Most people in Latin America and the Caribbean are **Christians**, but some people belong to religions that are based on beliefs that originally came from West Africa. Two examples are **santería**, a religion that is found in Cuba, and **candomblé**, a religion from Brazil. Music, especially drumming, is an important part of these religions.

Calling up the spirits

In both Cuba and Brazil, many of the slaves in the 19th century came from the Yoruba region of Nigeria. In the Yoruba religion, nature and human affairs are ruled over by spirits called *orishas*, who are messengers from God. *Santería* and *candomblé* are both based on Yoruba beliefs.

In a *santería* religious ceremony, drum music is used to call the spirits of the *orishas*. Each spirit has their own particular **rhythm**. A singer leads the entire group of worshipers to call the spirits. At times, the drumming and singing send some worshipers into a trance. This is a state in which they are not really aware of where they are or what they are doing. Worshipers believe that when they are in a trance, they are being visited by one of the spirits.

These drummers are playing for a *santería* ceremony in Cuba. *Santería* drumming is played on three double-headed hourglass shaped drums, called the *bata*.

The drum music played in *santería* and other religious ceremonies is very similar to African music. The drums themselves are similar to West African drums, and the drums play rhythms similar to those played in Nigeria.

In Cuba and Brazil, *santería* and *candomblé* drumming have spilled over into other types of music. At dances and celebrations, Cuban drummers play **rumba**, which is similar to *santería* music. In Brazil, *candomblé* drumming has developed into the best-known music of Brazil, **samba**.

Religious voodoo

Voodoo has a bad reputation. In movies and stories, people can be killed by voodoo. In fact *voudou* is a religious belief from Haiti that is similar to *santería* and *candomblé*. In *voudou* the spirits are known as *loas*. They are believed to be sent by God to help, protect, and guide people.

These drummers and dancers are at a *candomblé* ceremony in Rio de Janeiro, Brazil. Like *santería* worshipers, *candomblé* dancers sometimes go into a trance.

Carnivals and Festivals

The big event of the year in Brazil is Carnival. Every February the city of Rio de Janeiro has a four-day holiday, and the streets are filled with music and dancing. People parade through the streets in glittering costumes or ride on large decorated floats. But the most important groups of people in the Carnival parade are the **samba** bands.

Samba music

Samba is the most popular type of music in Brazil. At Carnival time, samba means drumming and dancing. During the rest of the year people play something known as song samba. This is quieter music for smaller groups to listen to on the radio or in cafés.

The samba bands that parade through the streets have hundreds of drummers. The large, deep *surdo* drums make such a loud noise that you can feel it through your entire body. There are also smaller drums, called **friction drums**, that make a strange squeaking sound, as well as rattles, scrapers, whistles, and small guitars.

People dance along with the parade, taking small steps and swaying their hips to the **rhythm**. They add to the sound by tapping out rhythms on bottles, cans, or anything else they can find. Over the top of all this, a singer sings new samba tunes that have been writen specfically for the Carnival.

Music duels

The Brazilian Carnival is not the only large music fiesta in Latin America. Other countries also have carnival-style festivals. In Peru, for instance, there is a festival called *Inti Raymi* (Festival of the Sun) in June. This involves dancing to street bands like at Carnival. At New Year festivals in some parts of Mexico, there are music duels between two bands set up on either side of the village square. Each band has a *trovatore* singer (a poet who makes up verses about anything from the stars and planets to local gossip). After a night of music-making, one of the bands admits defeat and the festival ends.

This is one of the samba bands in the samba parade in Rio de Janeiro. The competition to find the best samba band lasts for three days.

Caribbean carnivals

Carnivals are also important in the Caribbean. On many islands there is music specifically linked to carnivals. In Guadeloupe in the Antilles, musicians play *gwo ka* drum music, similar in style to samba. In Haiti, large **orchestras** play fast, sweet-sounding *compas* music. The biggest carnivals in the Caribbean take place in Trinidad.

Calypso carnivals

Calypso is more of a musical mixture than samba. It is based partly on songs that the French and Spanish brought to Trinidad. However, it did not stay in Trinidad. In the 1950s, many people from Trinidad and Jamaica **emigrated** to Great Britain to work. They brought Caribbean culture with them, especially calypso and carnival. From 1959 to 1964, small carnival celebrations were held in London in January. In 1964 the carnival was moved to Notting Hill in London. The new Carnival was held in August because January was too cold for a street festival. Today the Notting Hill Carnival is the largest street festival in Europe. More than a million people go there each year.

Calypso is also based partly on music that was played during stick fights. Fighting with light sticks was a popular sport with black slaves in Trinidad. It still takes place at carnival time. Stick fighting is a cross between boxing and fencing, all done to a rhythm.

When two stick fighters meet for a fight, each has a group of supporters, led by a singer called a chantwell. The chantwell's job is to sing about their fighter's skills and to make fun of the opponent. At carnival time, chantwells parade through the streets with a band and sing their songs.

These colorfully dressed drummers are performing at the Mardi Gras festival in New Orleans, Louisiana.

Calypso music has a bouncy rhythm that makes it fun to dance to. However, the most important part of a calypso is not the rhythm, but the words. Calypso songs are about all types of subjects. Singers might boast about their own skill or make fun of a rival singer. They might sing about current events or about famous people or politicians. Whatever a calypso is about, it is usually funny and sometimes rude!

During carnival time, there are calypso competitions. The person who sings the best calypso is crowned Calypso Monarch.

Mighty Sparrow is one of the greatest of all calypso singers. Here he is singing at a concert in New Orleans, Louisiana. He has won the Calypso Monarch award eight times.

Steel bands

Steel band music is another type of carnival music from Trinidad. Trinidad was ruled by the British from the late 1800s until 1962, when the country became independent. After the British rulers banned African-style drum music of all types, carnival bands in the late 1800s and early 1900s played pieces of hollow bamboo that they hit with sticks.

Bamboo did not make very good drums, so musicians began to experiment with other materials. Cookie tins, garbage can lids, and other pieces of metal began to replace bamboo.

In the 1940s, some players found that if they hammered the bottom of an oil drum, to make it dish-shaped, they could make drums that played several different notes.

Within a few years steel bands had become an essential part of the carnival in Trinidad. By the 1960s, the carnival had a separate competition for the best steel band. Steel bands soon became popular internationally.

Lots of pans

Steel drums are called pans. They come in different sizes, depending on whether they play high or low notes.

◎ Tenor lead pans play the highest notes. These shallow pans can have as many as 30 notes on one drum.

◎ Guitar and cello pans play in the middle range. Each pan has about six to eight notes. A player has two or three pans to get a full range of notes.

◎ Tenor bass pans play the lowest notes. There is only room for three or four notes on each pan. A player may have a set of six, nine, or even twelve bass pans.

This picture shows a steel band playing in Port of Spain, the capital of Trinidad.

Tango, Rumba, and Mambo

It is not just carnival music that is good to dance to. Many types of Latin and Caribbean popular music are made for dancing. During the 20th century, Latin-American dance music such as **tango**, **rumba**, **mambo**, and **salsa** became popular around the world.

Tango beginnings

The first Latin-American music to sweep the world was tango from Argentina and Uruguay. In the late 19th century, Argentina became rich from selling its beef and wheat around the world. The most popular music in Buenos Aires (the capital of Argentina) at this time was *milonga*. In the bars and cafés of the poorer areas of the city, everyone was dancing to *milonga*.

La Boca (the mouth) is the colorful port area of Buenos Aires. It is where tango first developed.

Some of the young white people dancing to the *milonga* began to copy movements from African-style dances that they saw black dancers doing. In these dances, the dancers would dance closely, but not touch one another. As part of the dance, they would pause, then make a sudden, dramatic movement. *Milonga* dancers copied these dramatic movements, but they danced in couples rather than alone.

At first, the musicians **improvised** to fit in with the new type of dancing. But soon a new type of music began to develop that fit with the dance style. Tango music was born.

A typical tango band includes a guitar, violin, doublebass, and *bandoneon* (accordion). At the heart of the music is an uneven, I–2 **rhythm**. The music and the dancing are fiery and passionate.

Button accordion

The *bandoneon* or button accordion is an essential part of any tango group. The *bandoneon* has 71 buttons, 38 for the right hand and 33 for the left. Each button produces two notes, one when pulling air into the *bandoneon* and the other when squeezing air out.

The tango craze

Early tango could be rough and downright rude. However, as it became more popular, a smoother style developed. By the early 1900s, tango was popular in much of Argentina and Uruguay.

Around 1910, several Argentinean musicians traveled to Paris to record tango music. The music and dancing was a hit in Paris high society. By 1913 tango fever had spread across Europe, and in 1914 it reached New York.

World War I put an end to the first tango boom. Most Argentinean musicians left Europe when the fighting started. However, after the war, tango became even more popular. During this time, tango's greatest singer, Carlos Gardel, rose to fame. In 1921, tango made it to Hollywood, when the movie star Rudolph Valentino danced the tango in a movie. In the 1930s, Carlos Gardel performed in several movies, including *Tango on Broadway* and *Tango Bar*.

After the 1930s, tango became less popular elsewhere, but it continued to be very popular in Argentina. Younger musicians such as Astor Piazzolla took tango in new directions. Piazzolla wrote complex tango music designed to be listened to in concerts, rather than as dance music. Today his music is often played by classical musicians. However, most tango is still dance music.

This picture shows dancers from Tango por Dos (Tango for Two), a dance company from Argentina. They perform shows about tango and its history in theaters around the world.

Carlos Gardel

Carlos Gardel (1893–1935) was born in France, but his mother moved to Buenos Aires when Carlos was only two. He loved the theater, and as a teenager he began entertaining people as a folk singer. In 1911, Carlos met another singer, José Razzano, and the two of them became very successful singers. However, in 1924 José developed a throat problem and had to stop singing. Carlos began to perform alone. For more than ten years Carlos was a tango superstar. He toured the world and recorded roughly 900 songs. In 1935, he was killed in an airplane crash.

Rumba and mambo

In Cuba in the 19th century, rumba was the favorite dance music among the slaves. Rumba developed from *santería* drumming, but it was a new type of music made in Cuba, not a copy of West African drumming. Rumba was important because it became the basis for many other types of Latin music.

The heart of rumba music is the rhythm that is played on a pair of hard sticks, known as claves. The clave rhythm is always the same in any rumba song. Clave rhythms are found in many types of Latin music. The singing in rumba is a call-and-response style of singing, with a lead singer singing one line or verse, and a chorus of singers responding.

In the 1920s, a new form of dance music, called *son* (short for *danzón*, or dance), grew out of rumba. *Son* has a rhythm similar to rumba, but it begins with a more European-style song, sung by one singer. After the song the music goes into a more open-ended section called the *montuno*. In this section the lead singer improvises (makes up) new lines and the chorus chimes in with a regular response.

Mambo

In the 1930s and 1940s, *son* became popular in the United States, and many Cuban musicians played there. The Cubans visiting the United States heard a lot of **jazz**, and this changed the way they played *son*. Bands became bigger, and each instrument had a specific part in the music.

Another new development was mambo. Mambo was jazzed-up, speeded-up *son* played by big bands. In the 1940s, the bandleader Pérez Prado made mambo the hottest sound in Havana, and in the 1950s it became a craze in New York. Mambo bands were in demand in every dance hall, and mambo dances were packed.

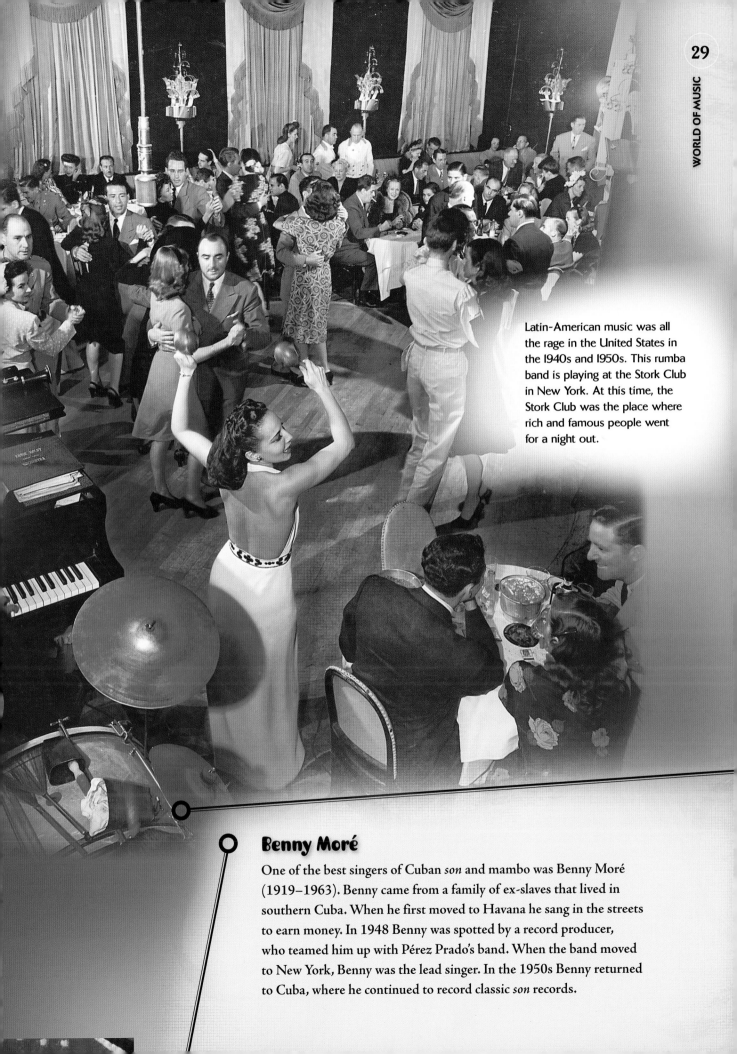

Latin-American music was all the rage in the United States in the 1940s and 1950s. This rumba band is playing at the Stork Club in New York. At this time, the Stork Club was the place where rich and famous people went for a night out.

Benny Moré

One of the best singers of Cuban *son* and mambo was Benny Moré (1919–1963). Benny came from a family of ex-slaves that lived in southern Cuba. When he first moved to Havana he sang in the streets to earn money. In 1948 Benny was spotted by a record producer, who teamed him up with Pérez Prado's band. When the band moved to New York, Benny was the lead singer. In the 1950s Benny returned to Cuba, where he continued to record classic *son* records.

Town and Country

S ome types of Latin-American music can sound similar to each other. **Salsa** can sound like **mambo**, and **samba** sounds similar to **bomba**.

Two styles that are very different from each other are ***bossa nova*** and Mexican *son*. Mexican *son* is originally a type of country dance music. A *son* tune will always liven things up. *Bossa nova* is city music. The tunes and the words are cool and sophisticated.

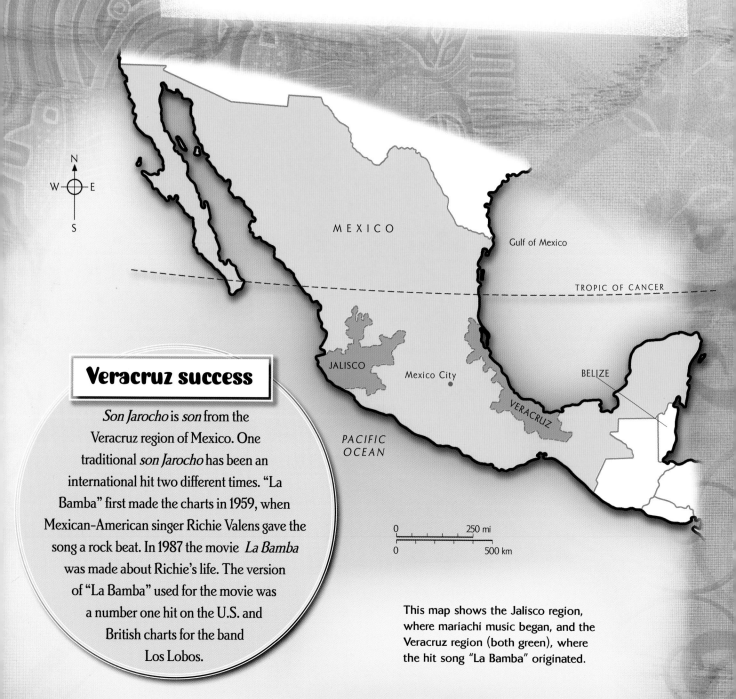

N
W—E
S

MEXICO

Gulf of Mexico

TROPIC OF CANCER

JALISCO

Mexico City

BELIZE

VERACRUZ

PACIFIC
OCEAN

0   250 mi
0   500 km

Veracruz success

Son Jarocho is *son* from the Veracruz region of Mexico. One traditional *son Jarocho* has been an international hit two different times. "La Bamba" first made the charts in 1959, when Mexican-American singer Richie Valens gave the song a rock beat. In 1987 the movie *La Bamba* was made about Richie's life. The version of "La Bamba" used for the movie was a number one hit on the U.S. and British charts for the band Los Lobos.

This map shows the Jalisco region, where mariachi music began, and the Veracruz region (both green), where the hit song "La Bamba" originated.

The sound of the country

Traditional Mexican *son* is dance music. The main instruments are guitars, harps, and violins. Part of the **rhythm** comes from the audience, who perform foot-stomping dances in times with the music. One type of *son*, from the Jalisco district, has become popular through groups known as *mariachi* bands. *Mariachi* bands have been popular at weddings and other celebrations since the 19th century. The musicians usually play guitars, violins, and more recently, trumpets.

Mariachi music was not well known outside of the Jalisco region until the 1930s. Then the band Mariachi Vargas was invited to play for President Cardenas (the Mexican president) in Mexico City. In the 1940s and 1950s *mariachi* music became popular in the United States. Mariachi Vargas appeared in many Hollywood movies and played with top movie stars.

Mariachi music is still popular in Mexico and parts of the United States. Many *mariachi* groups play in cafés and bars. Customers pay the musicians to play specific songs. The bands still play *son*, but they also play a wide range of other music. A good *mariachi* band will know roughly 1,500 different songs!

One unusual feature of a mariachi band is the range of different guitars. You can see from this picture that as well as playing normal guitars, the men are playing a small guitar called a *vilhuela*, and a huge bass guitar called a *guitarron*.

Brazilian cool

*B*ossa nova music developed in the mid-1950s in Rio de Janeiro in Brazil. The most important *bossa nova* musicians were Tom Jobím (real name Antonio Carlos Jobím) and João Gilberto. Tom was a pianist and **composer**. He grew up in Rio, listening to samba and other Brazilian music. He also trained as a classical musician. He was a fan of the Brazilian composer Heitor Villa-Lobos, who had combined the music of classical masters, such as Bach, with Brazilian **folk** music.

Tom began to write music that was based on samba, but had complex **harmonies** and simple, beautiful tunes. He teamed up with guitarist and singer João Gilberto, who added a gentle, swaying rhythm on the guitar. The two wrote the music for a very successful movie, *Black Orpheus*, and this helped make *bossa nova* music popular in Brazil.

In the early 1960s, North American jazz musicians such as saxophone player Stan Getz became interested in *bossa nova*. They recorded jazz albums that included *bossa nova* songs and rhythms. These records made the music popular across North America and Europe. Singing stars such as Ella Fitzgerald and Frank Sinatra made records of *bossa nova* hits.

The movie *Black Orpheus* made *bossa nova* music famous outside Brazil. It won the Oscar for best foreign film in 1960.

Bossa hits

Bossa nova songs such as *Desafinado* ("Out of Tune") and *Corcovado* ("Quiet Nights of Quiet Stars") have been chart hits. The biggest *bossa nova* hit was "The Girl from Ipanema." It was recorded by Stan Getz, João Gilberto, and João's wife Astrud. In 1964 it reached number two on the U.S. charts, and stayed on the charts for 96 weeks.

This picture shows Stan Getz playing the saxophone while Astrud Gilberto sings.

Protest Songs

Latin America and the Caribbean have had a troubled history. For more than 300 years the entire region was ruled from Europe, and many people were slaves. Once countries became independent, there was still great inequality. Large landowners became rich and powerful, but many poor people were not much better off than when they were slaves.

Some countries were ruled by **dictators**, who did not allow any type of complaint or **protest**. However, people did protest. One way that they did this was through music.

Spreading the word

Victor Jara was a 1960s musician from Chile who wrote songs that protested against his government. He was murdered because of this. This made musicians throughout Latin America feel unsafe. Many left for Europe. However, throughout the 1970s and 1980s, musicians such as Mercedes Sosa, Chico Buarque, and Chilean group Inti-Illimani traveled the world. They made *nueva canción* popular through political songs such as *Un pueblo unido Jamás Será vencido* ("The people, united, will never be defeated").

Mercedes Sosa is a singer from Argentina. She does not write songs herself, but she has sung *nueva canción* songs in concerts around the world. She has won three Grammy awards for her records, and is a United Nations Goodwill Ambassador.

These people are paying their respects to Victor Jara outside the National Stadium in Santiago, Chile. Each year Chilean people light candles in memory of Jara.

New songs

In the 1950s, a style of music known as *nueva canción* (new song) began to appear in Latin America. The music grew out of the work of two people—the Argentinean Atahualpa Yupanqui and the Chilean Violeta Parra.

In the 1950s, both Atahualpa and Violeta began writing and playing their own songs. These were a combination of Andean **folk** songs, Spanish music, and Latin-American **rhythms**. Some were sad songs about the difficulties of life for rural people. Others were angry songs that protested injustice.

In the 1960s, *nueva canción* became an important style across Latin America and the Caribbean. The best-known musicians included Victor Jara in Chile, Mercedes Sosa

in Argentina, Chico Buarque in Brazil, and Daniel Viglietti in Uruguay. The songs were beautiful tunes with poetic lyrics (words). However, they still managed to be political.

In 1970, the Chilean people voted in a new president, Salvador Allende. Victor Jara was a great supporter of President Allende, and wrote songs in praise of him. However, three years later Allende was overthrown when General Augusto Pinochet seized power.

Pinochet arrested hundreds of people who had supported President Allende, including Victor Jara. He was tortured and shot, then his body was dumped in the street. However, Jara lives on through his songs, which are still performed today.

A different sound

In the 1970s, Jamaica was the center of a very different type of protest music. This music was **reggae**.

Reggae began to develop in Jamaica in the 1960s. Before that time, the most popular type of Jamaican music was *mento*. *Mento* is lively, upbeat dance music that sounds like calypso. However, it has a different, shuffling type of rhythm.

In the 1950s, *mento* became less popular as Jamaicans began to listen to American **rhythm and blues** (**R&B**). During the 1960s, Jamaicans began to record their own versions of R&B records. At first these were just copies of the originals, but gradually the music changed to suit Jamaican tastes. The new version of R&B became known as *ska*.

Desmond Dekker was one of the first Jamaican musicians to be successful abroad. In 1968, his song "The Israelites" was a Top Ten hit in the United States and went to Number One on the British charts.

At first *ska* was local music, but it soon caught on in the United States and Great Britain. By 1965 there were millions of *ska* fans outside of Jamaica. In Kingston, the Jamaican capital, meanwhile, musicians were experimenting with the music. They slowed the beat down, and added in the shuffling rhythm from *mento*. The new sound was called reggae.

Ska was pure entertainment, but the same was not true of reggae. Reggae developed in the poor areas of Kingston, where there was often violence and injustice. Some reggae musicians urged poor people to "stand up for your rights" and speak out against injustice. They also protested against the violence and cruelty they saw in the world.

One of the early reggae groups was The Wailers (Bunny Wailer, Peter Tosh, and Bob Marley). Bob Marley was a superb songwriter and a powerful performer. In the early 1970s, he went from being a local Kingston musician to a reggae superstar. The clean, slightly rocky sound of Marley's reggae, and the message of his songs, appealed to people around the world.

Bob Marley is a reggae legend. Although he died in 1981, his records still sell in the millions. This photo is from a concert in 1978.

Bob Marley

The Wailers' earliest success, "Simmer Down" was about trying to calm down the violence in the Kingston **ghettos**. In 1974, Bob Marley (1945–1981) became a solo singer and had great success in the United States and Great Britain. In 1976 he was shot in an unsuccessful attempt to keep him from playing a concert promoting peace in Jamaican politics. He was forced to leave Jamaica for his own safety. However, he returned in 1978 for a concert that he called *One Love*, where he appealed for an end to violence.

A Latin Mix

Latin-American and Caribbean music such as **tango**, calypso, ***bossa nova***, and **reggae** have influenced music throughout the world, and the process has also worked in the opposite direction. Music such as **jazz**, **R&B**, rock, and **hip hop** have influenced what Latin-American and Caribbean musicians choose to play.

This is based partly on money. Latin or Caribbean musicians who do well in the United States and Europe will make more money than they could working in their home countries. However, it is also because musicians always want to create something new and original.

Salsa roots

Salsa is classic Latin-American music. However, salsa was not created in Latin America at all! Salsa developed in the late 1960s in New York.

New York has a large Latin-American population. Many of these Latin Americans originally came from Puerto Rico. From the 1930s to the 1950s, a steady stream of Cuban musicians brought *son*, **rumba**, **mambo**, and other Cuban music styles to New York.

In the early 1960s, the United States broke ties with the **communist** government in Cuba, because of its close ties with the Soviet Union, an enemy of the U.S. Some Cuban musicians moved permanently to the United States, but there was no new music from Cuba.

Latin musicians in New York turned to other music for ideas. They kept the basic structure of Cuban *son*, but added new things to it. They took **rhythms** and a high-**pitched** singing style from Puerto Rican music. They also added funky sounds and electric instruments from American soul music. The result was salsa.

Hot sauce

In cooking, salsa is a hot sauce. Salsa music is a hot mix of musical ingredients. Drums, claves, shakers, and scrapers play complex, overlapping rhythms, supported by piano or rhythm guitar. The tune goes back and forth between the lead singer and a chorus. A brass section (trumpets, trombones, and saxophones) often bursts in with short blasts of sound.

Salsa dancing has been around for 40 years and it is still wildly popular. These salsa fans are at a dance in London.

Salsa spreads

By the mid-1970s, salsa was the most popular music in Latin America, especially in Cuba and Puerto Rico. But the success of salsa did not stop there. Salsa began to gain a large following around the world. Latin-American musicians such as Celia Cruz, Eddie Palmieri, Willie Colón, and Rubén Blades were international stars.

The Cuban guitarist Compay Segundo (left) and American Ry Cooder playing with Buena Vista Social Club in 1998. Compay played a seven-string guitar that he invented, called an *armonico*. He was 91 when this photograph was taken.

The success of salsa led to the popularity of other types of Latin dance music. The large numbers of Latin Americans living in the United States also helped. **Merengue** from the Dominican Republic and **zouk** from the Antilles have become almost as popular as salsa.

Lambada is a mix of musical ideas from Bolivia and the Amazon region of Brazil. The music, and the dance style that went with it, were picked up by French music producers and turned into an international craze.

Since the 1970s, there has been a lot of crossover between Latin-American, Caribbean, and other types of music. For example, beginning in the early 1970s reggae record producers were creating dubbed versions of reggae songs. These were the instrumental parts from reggae songs with echo and other effects added.

Dub tracks were used by DJs to "toast" (talk over the music) at dances. In the late 1970s, African-Americans in New York began to use similar ideas, which developed into **rap** and hip hop music.

Son explosion

Salsa is based on Cuban *son*, which was first popular in the 1940s and 1950s. But in 1997, an album came out that made *son* world famous. The album was made by the American guitarist Ry Cooder, who went to Cuba in 1996 to play with *son* musicians. He gathered together a group of experienced musicians who had played *son* in the 1940s and 1950s. The album that the group made was called *Buena Vista Social Club*, after a Havana club that was popular in the 1950s. It sold more than two million copies worldwide. In 2003, *Buena Vista* was voted one of the top 500 albums of all time by *Rolling Stone* magazine.

Unusual mixes

But that is not the end of the story. Latin-American and Caribbean musicians have taken ideas from rap and hip hop music to create new versions of old styles. Puerto Rico, for instance, is the home of Latin rap, while in Trinidad rap has been combined with calypso to produce *rapso*. And a new kind of Spanish reggae, known as *reggaeton*, is rapidly becoming one of the most popular new music styles in Latin America and the Caribbean.

Rock music is another music style that has been picked up by Latin musicians. In the 1960s and 1970s, Latin rock mostly copied rock styles from the United States or Great Britain. More recently, however, bands have brought Latin sounds into rock. Café Tacuba and Los de Abajo from Mexico, and Bloque from Colombia, are among the most popular bands in Latin rock.

Reggaeton star Daddy Yankee (right) with rapper P. Diddy (Sean Combs) at a concert in 2005. Daddy Yankee is one of the most successful *reggaeton* artists.

Chutney music

Some newer types of Latin and Caribbean music bring in sounds from unexpected places. One surprising combination comes from Trinidad. In the 1970s, traditional calypso was joined by a louder, faster, party sound called *soca*. Asians living in Trinidad combined Indian instruments and singing with a *soca* beat to make music known as chutney. In the words of one chutney song:

> **Indian music, sounding sweeter,**
>
> **hotter than a chulha [*a stove*].**
>
> **Rhythm from Africa and India,**
>
> **blending together in a perfect mixture.**

Keeping the roots alive

With so much mixing and copying of styles, musicians could easily lose connection with the music of their own country. However, since they have become independent, Latin-American and Caribbean countries have taken great pride in their **folk** music. Many new styles are being created, but traditional ones are also going strong. The best types of modern Latin and Caribbean music have something new to say, but they keep a connection to old traditions.

Chutney music is a mixture of traditional Indian folk music with *soca* rhythms. These chutney performers are taking part in the Chutney *soca* finals at the Trinidad Carnival in 2004.

RENT -A -AMP

A World of Music

	String Instruments	Brass Instruments	Wind Instruments
Africa	*oud* (lute), *rebec* (fiddle), *kora* (harp-lute), *ngoni* (harp), musical bow, one-string fiddle	*kakaki* or *wazi* (metal trumpets), horns made from animal horns	*naga, nay sodina* (flutes), *arghul, gaita* (single-reed instruments), *mizmar* (double-reed instrument)
Australia, Hawaii, and the Pacific	ukulele (modern), guitar (modern)		flutes, nose flutes, didjeridus, conch shell horns
Eastern Asia	*erhu* (fiddle), *dan tranh, qin, koto, gayageum* (derived from *zithers*)	gongs, metallophones, xylophones	*shakuhachi* (flute), *khaen* (mouth organ), *sralai* (reed instrument)
Europe	violin, viola, cello, double bass, mandolin, guitar, lute *zither*, hurdy gurdy (folk instruments)	trumpet, French horn, trombone, tuba	flute, recorder, oboe, clarinet, bassoon, bass clarinet, saxophone, accordion, bagpipes
Latin America and the Caribbean	*berimbau* (musical bow), *guitarrón* (bass guitar), *charango* (mandolin), *vilhuela* (high-pitched guitar)	trumpet, saxophone, trombone (salsa instruments)	*bandoneon* (button accordion)
Western Asia	*sitar, veena, oud, dombra, doutar, tar* (lutes), *rebab, kobyz* (fiddles), *sarod, santoor, sarangi*	trumpets	*bansuri, ney* (flutes), *pungi/been* (clarinets) *shehnai, sorna* (oboes)

Percussion Instruments	Vocal Styles	Dance Styles
balafon (wooden xylophone), *mbira* (thumb piano), bells, slit drums, friction drums, hourglass drums, conventional drums	open throat singing, Arabic-style singing: this is more nasal (in the nose), and includes many trills and ornaments	spiritual dancing, mass dances, team/formation dances, small group and solo dances, modern social dances
slit drums, rattles, drums, clapsticks, gourds, rolled mats	*oli* (sung by one person), *mele* (poetry), hula, *himene* (choral music), dreaming songs	hula, seated dances, *fa'ataupati* (clapping and slapping), haka
taiko (drums)	*p'ansori* (single singer), *chooimsae* (verbal encouragement), folk songs	Peking/Beijing opera, Korean folk dance
side drum, snare drum, tambourine, *timpani* (kettle drums), cymbals, castanets, bodhran, piano	solo ballad, work song, hymn, plainchant, opera, Music Hall, cabaret, choral, homophony (**harmony**, parts moving together), polyphony (independent vocals together)	jig, reel, sword dance, clog dance, *mazurka* (folk dances), flamenco, country dance, waltz, polka, ballet, *pavane, galliard* (1500s)
friction drum, steel drums, bongos (small drums), congas (large drums), *timbales* (shallow drums), maracas (shakers), *guiro* (scraper)	toasting	*zouk* (pop music), tango, lambada, samba, *bossa nova* (city music), rumba, mambo, *merengue* (salsa)
tabla drum, *dhol* drum, tambourine, *bartal* cymbals, bells, sticks, gongs	bards, *bhangra* (Punjabi), *qawwali* (Sufi music), throat singing, *ghazals* (love poems)	*bhangra, dabke* (traditional dances), Indian classical, whirling dervishes, belly dancing

Glossary

Amerindian short for "American Indian." Any of the native people who lived in North or South America before Europeans arrived.

armadillo South American animal that is covered in a bony armor shell

bomba type of music from Puerto Rico, played on short, fat drums called bombas.

bossa nova cool, jazzy style of music from Brazil that first became popular in the 1960s

candomblé religion that was brought to Brazil from West Africa by slaves

Christian someone who believes that Jesus Christ was the son of God

colony place ruled by people from another country

communism economic system in which the government owns and runs everything

composer person who writes music

dictator ruler who has all the power in a country and crushes any opposition

emigrate to move from a person's country of birth to live in a new country

folk traditional music of a specific area

friction drum drum that is played by rubbing the skin instead of hitting it

ghetto part of a city where a minority group lives. It is usually a deprived area.

harmony combination of similar musical notes

hip hop type of American urban (city) music in which DJs talk rhythmically over a music track or other background music

improvise make up the words to a song or piece of music

jazz type of American popular music that has strong rhythms and is based on improvisation (making up music on the spot)

mambo fast, jazz-style Cuban music and dance style that was popular in the 1950s

mandolin small stringed instrument similar to a guitar, with four pairs of strings

merengue originally a type of dance music from the Dominican Republic. Today merengue is a style of music often played by salsa groups.

orchestra large group of trained musicians playing a range of instruments

panpipes set of several hollow tubes of different lengths that produce different notes when you blow over the top of them

percussion drums and other types of instruments that you hit, scrape, or shake to make sounds

pitch "highness" or "lowness" of a note. A scream is generally high-pitched, the rumble of thunder is low-pitched.

protest to publicly disagree with the actions of someone else. Most protests are political.

rap type of music in which rhyming and rhythmic words are spoken over background music

reggae type of Jamaican music with a strong bass and an off-beat rhythm

rhythm beat behind a piece of music

rhythm and blues (R&B) American style of pop music from the 1940s that was the forerunner of rock 'n' roll

rumba African-style, Cuban dance music. Rumba is also a Latin-American ballroom dance style.

salsa type of Latin-American music and dancing from New York

samba loud drum music from Brazil

santería religion that was brought to Cuba from West Africa by slaves

soundtrack music from a movie

Taino Indians part of a group of Amerindians who lived in Jamaica, Cuba, Haiti, and the Dominican Republic around the 15th century

tango type of music and a dance from Argentina that has become popular worldwide

zouk high-energy pop music from the Antilles in the Caribbean

Further Information

Books

Brunning, Rob and Pickering, James. *World Music (Sound Trackers)*. Chicago: Heinemann Library, 2003.

Jacobs, Hiedi Hayes. *World Studies: Latin America*. Upper Saddle River, N.J. Pearson Prentice Hill, 2005.

Kallen, Stuart A. *The History of Latin Music*. New York: Lucent Books, 2006.

Websites

Bitesize African and Caribbean music
www.bbc.co.uk/schools/gcsebitesize/music/worldmusic/africanandcaribbeanrevl.shtml

Bitesize Latin American music
www.bbc.co.uk/schools/gcsebitesize/music/worldmusic/latinamericanrevl.shtml

Calabash Music
http://news.calabashmusic.com/world/getstarted

National Geographic World Music
http://worldmusic.nationalgeographic.com/worldmusic/view/page.basic/home

Smithsonian Global Sound
www.smithsonianglobalsound.org

Sound Junction
www.soundjunction.org/default.aspa

Places to visit

Mardi Gras, New Orleans, Louisiana
Hundreds of thousands of tourists visit New Orleans every year in February or March for what has been called "the greatest free show on Earth."
www.mardigrasday.com

Dancing
Resorts, workshops, and other tango activities of international interest. Includes U.S. tango festivals.
www.tangofestivals.net

Home of the annual World Salsa Championship Competition.
www.worldsalsachampionships.com

Bands
You could join a samba band, or at least go and listen to one. There are samba bands all over the world. Look in your local library to find your nearest band.

Index